THE PSYCHOLOGY OF CONSPIRACY THEORISTS

Written by

Dr. Austin Mardon, Terrence Wu,

Ashmita Mazumder, Haya Sonawala

Khushi Shah, Iqra Abid, & Anna Yang

Edited by

Kathryn Carson & Taryn Foster

GM★ PRESS

Typeset and Cover Design by Kim Huynh

ISBN 978-1-77369-607-2
EBook ISBN 978-1-77369-608-9

Golden Meteorite Press
103 11919 82 St NW
Edmonton, AB T5B 2W3
www.goldenmeteoritepress.com

GM★
P R E S S

Table of Contents

The Psychology of Conspiracy Theorists

The term "conspiracy theory" is becoming alarmingly prevalent in our current media landscape. But what does that actually mean? What are conspiracy theories and how do they burrow their way into our society and influence so many people, potentially even changing their fundamental beliefs and world views? These are the questions The Psychology of Conspiracy Theorists seeks to explore. In order to situate our reader, this discussion begins with the impact of conspiracy theories in our modern world and an in-depth breakdown of the definition and categorization of conspiracy theories. The following chapters will discuss the sweeping consequences of misinformation and two potential reasons why people believe in these theories despite the lack of scientific evidence to support them, specifically the existential and social motives behind their beliefs. This examination would be incomplete without exploring the origins and impacts of specific theories throughout recent history, including those surrounding the moon landing, 9/11, and even the now infamous virus COVID-19. The Psychology of Conspiracy Theorists strives to educate the general reader on the origins and the wide-reaching impacts of conspiracy theories as well as the psychology behind why people believe the unbelievable.

CHAPTER 1

Conspiracy theories in our modern world

Written by Terrence Wu

Introduction to Conspiracy Theories

A conspiracy theory is an ideology that challenges the belief systems set by an influential organization. There are many conspiracy theories that are spread throughout the media (online and offline) and are widely accepted by the global population. Conspiracy theories are commonly associated with "prejudice, witch hunts, revolutions, and genocide."[1] These ideas and belief systems can be very strong influences, leading people to believe a variety of facts that simply aren't true. This way of thinking benefits from the structure of certain mediums and communities, and in contemporary society, the internet is chief among them. What is more, conspiracy theories have developed surrounding the evolution and use of the internet. Based on our current knowledge of conspiracy theories, researchers believe that "the Internet was made for conspiracy theory: it is a conspiracy theory: one thing leads to another, always another link leading you deeper into no thing and no place."[2] For example, the large quantity of misinformation capable of spreading through the internet can undermine trust and belief in mainstream medicine. This has many implications for many global and public health initiatives, as once curable diseases are resurfacing among our populations. The prevalence of conspiracy theories has also led people to reject the scientific consensus on anthropogenic climate change despite the wide body of literature. It has also been found that "many perpetrators of terrorist attacks were known to be keen supporters of conspiracy theories."[1]

Types of Conspiracy Theories

There are many types of conspiracy theories in different fields of study, including "psychology, political science, sociology, history, information sciences, and humanities."[1] There are many topics covered within these areas of study, including science, health, the environment, immigration, racism, terrorism, politics, and international relations. Popular media has covered many famous examples of conspiracy theories, including those surrounding 9/11, the assassination of JFK, and the death of Princess Diana. Through publishing news articles, blog posts, and journals, there has also been a great deal of online discussion surrounding the moon landing and vaccine efficacy. The Internet has become a great tool for people to use, browse, and discuss their ideas. Online forums also provide opportunities for people to share their opinions, which "provides an excellent opportunity for archival research to give some insight into the thoughts and beliefs of those writing them."[3] Researchers can use this information to examine psychological states and thought patterns of human subjects that may be leading to the increasing emergence and prevalence of conspiracy theories.

Communicating Conspiracy Theories

Conspiracy theories can be communicated and shared in a variety of ways. For example, large social events, such as big-scale protests, can lead to the prevalence of conspiracy talk. These types of conventions allow people to congregate together which facilitates the transmission of knowledge. When people gather together, they usually have something in common with other people at the event which allows them to spark conversation among each other. For example, at a concert or music festival, people go to these types of events because they are fans of the musicians performing. In contrast, when people go to the mall, they usually don't in large groups, as everyone is there for a different reason. We typically don't go out of our way to speak to random strangers, even though we are all congregated together in one location. As previously mentioned, the Internet has a great deal of power by facilitating the rapid spread of large quantities of information over a remarkably short period of time. It has been found that "the speed of dissemination may even retard the progress of conspiracy theories into coherent arguments."[1] The types of conspiracy theories that get communicated tend to be quite drastic from public belief, which is a reason why it is so easy for people to adopt these new ideologies. In addition, the internet also has the power to reduce the amount of conspiracy theories being surfaced online "since billions of potentially critical voices are available to immediately refute conspiracy claims with evidence."[4] Later on in this chapter, the pros and cons of easy-access to knowledge and how this can lead to the translation of knowledge as well as the spread of misinformation among people will be discussed.

Researchers are currently investigating other intrinsic or extrinsic motivations within people that may influence discussions about conspiracy theories. Political perspectives can be extremely influential in altering a person's original assumptions about a particular belief system. From a political standpoint, "conspiracy narratives are used to dispute dominant political and ideological assumptions."[1] Ideological assumptions don't challenge public perception, and they are typically based on sound and logical evidence. There are also psychological motivations to influence a person's belief in certain conspiracy theories. Conspiracy theories tend to be formed when people are trying to understand or make sense of events that threaten existing worldviews or those that challenge our current belief system. The social representations theory is based on a system of beliefs and methodologies that people use to establish social order within their environment. People commonly draw on the social representations theory to create associations and "symbolically cope with threatening events by making abstract risk more concrete."[1]

The Arts and Media sector also has strong influences towards the development and spread of conspiracy theories. Social media and news outlets are popular avenues for information transmission in the modern world. There is also a wide array of films, known as "conspiracy cinema" that depicts our understanding of conspiracy theories through motion pictures. There are many misbeliefs associated with the music industry, from famous billboard artists to rock legends. Music with lyrics has also become a powerful tool for communicating conspiracy theories. Popular bands include Muse and White Power music.[5]

The Spread of Misinformation

The spread of misinformation—information or theories that are not supported by scientific evidence—through mainstream media and other information-rich sources has the ability to cause damage to audiences worldwide. The impacts of misinformation are drastic, from falsely understanding medical advice to political concerns. There is no doubt that technology has made information transmission much easier. However, it is also important to consider the effect of automated processes in a busy world. Technology offers a great deal of convenience to people working under tight schedules and deadlines. However, despite the integral role of technology in our society, it unfortunately allows for mistakes and errors that often go unrecognized until it's too late. Therefore, it is important to consider the impact of implementing technology in every aspect of our everyday life.

Just over a decade ago, there was a huge backlash over Andrew Wakefield and colleagues as they had previously published an article in the Lancet, a high-quality scientific research journal. The research paper was originally published in 1998, however, when it was published, it gained a significant degree of public media attention and tons of readers worldwide. This paper put forward the theory that the measles, mumps, and rubella vaccine (MMR) causes autism, as it links to behavioural regression and pervasive developmental disorder in children. Upon further investigation, there were many problems and ethical issues that Wakefield et al. (1998) faced as a result of conducting and publishing this study. The researchers did not receive ethics approval for how they were sampling and collecting data from children. There was also an incredibly small sample size (n=12 participants), uncontrolled study design, and speculative conclusions, among many other problems. Consequently, the study was retracted in February 2010 after many epidemiological studies were conducted and researchers were not able to come to the same conclusions as Wakefield et al. (1998). This discrepancy was due to the fact that they were selective of data and only picked cases that could support the results they wanted to publish. Additionally, it was found that they falsified many of their stated facts for financial gain. As a result, Andrew Wakefield, the lead investigator of this study, was found guilty of deliberate fraud.

The implications of this case were significant, as parents became hesitant to vaccinate their children with the MMR vaccine, despite the fact that it was already scientifically-proven to be ethical and safe by earlier research. Wakefield's study was singled out and seen as a large "blip" in the chain of knowledge translation, as it supported parents and caregivers who were hesitant to follow the advice of medical professionals to vaccinate and protect their children from developing measles, mumps, and rubella. Parents were fearful and believed the findings of Wakefield's study stating that the MMR vaccine causes autism, however, it took a great degree of convincing for the general public to believe that Wakefield's claims were indeed false and not scientifically backed by evidence. This scandal demonstrated the importance of being ethically responsible to ensure the highest standards of research design, data collection, data analysis, data reporting, and interpretation of findings. The purpose of which is to ensure the safety and protection of our global population, as "there can be no compromises because any error, any deceit, can result in harm to patients as well [as] jar, to the cause of science."[6]

The Importance of Proper Knowledge Translation

As most people are daily users of the Internet, there is a heightened importance in understanding the value of true information in an online age. When publishing journal articles or sharing new information, there are many ethical concerns to consider.[7] For example, if researchers decide to collect raw data from human participants, they will need to gain ethics approval from the Research Ethics Board (REB). The research study will need to be planned accordingly to specify details regarding how these researchers wish to collect data from their participants, while not causing any physical, psychological, or emotional harm. Subject participants will need to receive voluntary consent and understand the risks that they could experience as a result of being a participant in the study. Participant should feel free to withdraw from the study at any time, for any reason that does not need to be specified. They should not feel obliged to respond in ways that may be influenced by the researcher's behaviour.

The value of true information is linked to understanding the validity, reliability, and accuracy of the data being collected. There are relationships that need to be further examined once an association between the study theory and hypothesis have been made, which ties in existing concepts and indicators, as well as empiric data and analysis. The validity of information assesses the "relevance and appropriateness [of information] to your research question and the directness and strength of its association with the concepts under scrutiny".[7] Reliability in data is very important, as strong reliability builds more dependable and trustworthy relationships and associations that directly follows what the data suggests. The main measure of reliability is consistency in measuring and collecting data. Data accuracy is sensitive to change, due to the amount of detail that may be required in certain datasets. These details can include dates, numbers, units, location, etc.[7] All together, the validity, reliability, and accuracy of data allow for increased confidence that standard protocols and regulations are being followed when interpreting collected data and publishing findings made in research. These characteristics allow for the ability to reproduce original data and findings to secure the same results, truth and integrity of the research being conducted.

The Emergence of Conspiracy Theories in our Modern World

It has been believed that the Internet and social media is responsible for the rapid influx of conspiracy theories spiralling our everyday lives. To better understand this phenomena and its effect on the public, a group of researchers measured the impact of respondents believing the information in conspiracy theories that they encountered through surveys. Research scholars created scales to assess how much people believed the conspiracy theories they were faced with, and they were questioned to determine whether the respondents believed if these events had actually happened in real life. These surveys also included scales that were designed to measure the general tendency towards conspiracy thinking styles.[1] These were included to help researchers to determine what types of individuals want to challenge society the most? They hypothesize that these types of thinkers could generate conspiracy theories more readily than others.

Scholars have long hypothesized how conspiracy theories originated and dominated many facets of our modern life. It is believed that the development of conspiracy theories have some underlying roots in psychological sciences. Other theorists believe that "while many conceptually distinct conspiracy theories exist, the tendency to believe in them appears to be underpinned by broader beliefs that support conspiracy theories in general (e.g., beliefs in cover ups)."[8] It is also believed that conspiracy theories can be easily spun out of context due to social influences. This is very commonly seen in politics, as ideological motivations can influence election results.[8] The impact of conspiracy theories on our modern world has been substantial, which is partially due to the beliefs that are easily adopted by our global population.

There has been a great deal of speculation as to why conspiracy theories are so easily adopted by the general population. It is easy for people to believe facts without being supported by scientific evidence. However, understanding the whole truth (or backstory) that lends itself to the fact is also extremely important. This creates the distinction between understanding facts and truth. Facts are the available data -- they are not to be questioned. Truth is the reality behind the facts -- not everything is truly as it seems and outsider perspectives may not see the full picture, that is known as real life.[7] There is some scientific evidence to potentially explain why people believe in the conspiracy theories that are exploited around the world. There are natural human tendencies to believe anything that satisfies our preconceptions, whether they turn out to be true or not.

People tend to cognitive shortcuts that help them make decisions faster in a short period of time. However, as mentioned, these decisions can be detrimental which can have many large-scale effects.[9] These beliefs can cause general confusion and a loss of identity among individuals.

Conclusion

Our modern world is surrounded by conspiracy theories. These belief systems are typically set in place by our natural human desire to make quick-witted decisions to fill in cognitive gaps in our current understanding and knowledge. These choices can lead to the spread of misinformation and knowledge translation imbalances. If these ideas are taken way out of context, they can have detrimental effects on human health and well-being. Strong implications of misinformation include people rejecting publicly advertised medical advice, such as vaccine administration and practicing safe personal hygiene. It is important to stop the spread of conspiracy thinking because misinformation can cause damage to people's perceptions of their mental health and well-being.

CHAPTER 2

What exactly is a conspiracy theory?

Written by Ashmita Mazumder

Throughout history, the popularity of conspiracy theories has been widespread. Historically, these theories have been associated with witch hunts, genocide and prejudice.[5] The popularity of conspiracy theories can be attributed to the basic human instincts that allow people to adapt and evolve with their changing environments.[1] Conspiracy theories are a way for people to question actions or behavior that appear suspicious to them. In situations of ambiguity, conspiracy theories can provide explanations which appear appealing and settle unrest.[7] Such theories can spread through people, media or the internet. Sometimes, the hidden motive behind spreading a conspiracy theory is to manipulate and provoke people into siding with a particular belief.[7] This can lead to changes in either political or social opinion.

Everyone has a general idea of what a conspiracy theory is; however, there seems to be a disconnect between its definition and its applicability. Everything from the flat-earth theory to the anti-vaccine theory has been termed as a conspiracy. However, the term 'conspiracy theory' has a significantly different meaning than 'conspiracy'. Where conspiracy alludes to a secretive plan between two or more people, a conspiracy theory refers to a "hypothesized conspiracy with specific characteristics."[19] It is important to carefully understand and conceptualize conspiracy theories, as information can be taken out of context and defined as a conspiracy due to misrepresentation. An absence of distinctions between actual plots and conspiracies can cause errors in behaviors and lead to misguided thinking and hinder the larger conversation surrounding conspiracy theories and their impact.

Conspiracy theory has taken up multiple definitions. Some studies have regarded conspiracy theories as "explanatory beliefs about a group of people that meet in secret to reach malicious goals."[9] Others have defined conspiracy theories as "attempts to explain the ultimate cause of events as secret plots by powerful groups rather than overt activities or natural occurrences."[14] While these definitions fit the category of conspiracies that arise from historical events or pop culture, conspiracy theories surrounding political agendas are defined as "the ever present threat, rare in some places and more common in others to usurp the government."[1] The existence of multiple definitions hints at the debate that exists about the true definition of conspiracy theories. In colloquial terms, a "conspiracy theory" can be any small or large event that was carried out in secret by a group of people. Hence, the applicability of each definition varies with the situation it is applied to.

Conspiracies usually start as a suspicion.[8] Then, any evidence that supports their suspicions is regarded as proof and is forced to fit the theory. They can be hard to refute as anyone who tries is seen as taking part in the belief that the theory is trying to refute. No matter the definition, all conspiracy theories have six things in common. Firstly, they refer to an alleged and secret plot.[8] As the name suggests, conspiracies are carried out in secret without the knowledge of the general public. Hence, people that believe in such conspiracies think that they have some secret knowledge on how the world works. Let's consider the conspiracy theory regarding climate change. Believers of this conspiracy think that climate change was introduced to manipulate people's decisions on how to live their lives. Supporters of climate change encourage the use of renewable resources and recyclable products over others. Conspiracy theorists misunderstand these suggestions as attempts to manipulate their choices and violate their free will. According to these theorists, climate change is not what it seems; instead it is a secret plot for the government to control its citizens.

Secondly, these theories involve a group of conspirators.[8] Most theories that are termed conspiracy theories involve a large group of people that are trying to manipulate public opinion. Again, let's consider the conspiracy theory regarding climate change. Believers of this conspiracy theory believe that climate change is not real and that scientists and politicians are trying to manipulate our decisions by showcasing one-sided information. Here, all the scientists and all the politicians who support climate change are regarded as complicit in the hoax.

Thirdly, the theorists often have 'evidence' that seems to support their conspiracy theory.[8] This evidence can be in the form of beliefs or misconstrued notions. Going back to the example on climate change, any authors of scientific articles or news journals that seem to support climate change are regarded as part of the conspiracy. They are labeled as conspirators and part of the propaganda and their findings are disregarded. On the other hand, if any scientific article seems to confirm their suspicions then it is taken as evidence that their beliefs were correct after all.

Next, they falsely suggest that there are no coincidences, and that supports the theory is due to chance.[8] Conspiracy theorists believe that everything is related and nothing is as simple as it appears. They often believe there is some hidden motive for all behavior. For example, scientists and politicians that support climate change have a hidden motive for doing so, and even disparate behaviour may be linked back to the theory.

Fifth, they divide the world into good or bad.[8] As previously stated, conspiracy theorists believe that every action has a hidden motive and since nothing is a coincidence, people should be understood to have malevolent goals that they carry out in secret. In the case of the climate change conspiracy, theorists believe that either there are people who believe in the conspiracy and therefore make up the more knowledgeable and responsible group of society (the good). Conversely, there are people who do not believe in the theory, the ones that are manipulated and the conspirators themselves (the bad). Theorists do not consider people that do not have an opinion on the topic or the ones that consider both sides of the argument and decide to remain neutral on the topic.

Finally, they scapegoat people and groups.[8] Conspiracy theories provide a sense of superiority. As they seem to present some secret and valuable information, people are drawn to believe them. They are framed as lucrative, as believing in the theory also means that you are part of the secret and elite group that holds confidential knowledge. People who do not engage in rational thinking can often fall into the trap of believing these conspiracies.

Categories of conspiracy theories:

In addition to defining the term, researchers have also started to categorize different conspiracy theories into broader themes.

Micheal Barkun identified three classes of conspiracy theories:[19]

1. Event conspiracy theories: These theories are founded on well-defined events with specific characteristics. For example, the Kennedy assasination.

2. Systemic conspiracy theories: These theories surround beliefs about a group of people engaging in actions to fulfill their broader goals.

3. Superconspiracy theories: Theories that link multiple conspiracies together hierarchically.

More recently, researcher and author Jesse Walker has identified five types of conspiracy theories:[15]

1. The Enemy Without: A foreign figure's schemes against a community

2. The Enemy Within: Schemes against the nation by someone who is indistinguishable from others belonging to the same community

3. The Enemy Above: Manipulations by authority figures on the general public

4. The Enemy Below: Schemes by the lowest class of society for overthrowing social order

5. Benevolent conspiracies: Beliefs that supernatural powers are looking over humans and improving the lives of humans.

Conspiracy theories are notorious for being based on unfounded evidence and highly subjective thinking and beliefs.[6] Conversely, empirical research is based on the scientific method, which involves asking a question, doing background research, forming predictions based on research, testing with an experiment and updating initial beliefs on the topic. This process is repeated by multiple researchers for the same topic for it to be established as reliable information. Here, the purpose is to reject the null hypothesis, where the null hypothesis states that there is no real effect. Functionally, the goal behind knowledge backed up by research is to prove beyond reasonable doubt that the hypothesis is true. Therefore, scientific evidence is accepted after multiple rounds of investigation and experimentation. Even then, the scientific community is quick to criticize and constantly find ways to improve existing results. Conspiracy theories, in most cases, are based on fear or motivations that cannot be changed by rational arguments.This can be seen in the widespread 'anti-vaccination' theory where vaccinations are linked to autism and they are believed to contain chips that the government can use to track us.[13] Here, conspiracy theorists do not consider the extensive body of literature on this topic or the rigorous standards applied to scientific investigation. Any scientific evidence that suggests otherwise is regarded as political propaganda. However, if a scientific article states the opposite and confirms the suspicions of the conspiracy theorist, the results are declared to finally uncover the truth.[6] Due to application of this circular logic, most people are wary of challenging conspiracy theories.

Confirmation-Disconfirmation Bias

Believers of conspiracy theories often engage in a cognitive process known as the confirmation-disconfirmation bias. This cognitive theory explains that people compare the performance of a product with their conscious or unconscious opinions on its expected performance.[14] For example, if someone believes that the new toaster they bought will not work as well as the last one they had, it will affect the way they perceive the actual performance of the new toaster. Similarly, conspiracy theorists have suspicions about behaviors or actions around them which affects the way they perceive information. This is why it is difficult to break the loop of conspiracy theories as people need to be motivated to challenge their own perceptions about how things work in the world. However, researchers have conducted studies which investigate the likelihood of someone believing in a conspiracy.

Research has found that people are more likely to endorse conspiracy theories in situations of ambiguity and when they are looking for closure.[13] For example, the COVID-19 pandemic has brought on a surge of conspiracy theories which are mostly motivated by the need to explain uncertain situations.[5] Research has also found that people that endorsed conspiracy theories were more likely to conspire themselves.[4] Conspiracy beliefs were also associated with greater religious beliefs and greater beliefs in paranormal activity[3] and believing in one conspiracy also makes one more likely to believe in others.[10,11] People may also believe in conspiracy theories to improve their feelings while having this personal knowledge in a world full of opinions can also feel very empowering.[13] In recent years, social media has aided the spread of conspiracy theories by changing the way people share and access information. Now more than ever, it has become easier to share information found on the web which is then readily available for all to access. Referring to the example of climate change as a conspiracy theory, we can clearly see how misinformation on the internet has fueled its spread and increased support. Articles that deny climate change, written by self-proclaimed experts are shared at an alarmingly faster rate than scientific articles with well-founded evidence.[18] One of the reasons for this bias could be the readability of scientific articles. Such papers are written by academics and for academics. Hence, the general public can find it a bit hard to understand. On the other hand, articles written by conspiracy theorists are written in a subjective tone with anecdotes and examples from real life which people can relate to easily. Therefore, when there is a lack of motivation to understand (on the part of the reader) and lack of determination to make science more accessible (on the part of the scientific community) we can see why readers may prefer conspiracy theories over something that is not so easy to understand. As it becomes harder to access scientific articles, it becomes easier to fall for a theory found on the internet.

Steps to spot a conspiracy theory:

There are a few signs that readers can look out for to spot a conspiracy theory. Firstly, it is likely to be a conspiracy theory if the author claims to be an expert but is not attached to any recognized institute and has no qualifications or credentials on the topic.[8] If the author uses verifiable facts and evidence, the theory is less likely to be a conspiracy. Next, if the source of the conspiracy has been quoted by several media outlets or academics, it is less likely to be a conspiracy. However, if the source is unclear or only shared by self-proclaimed experts then readers should be wary of its reliability. Additionally, readers can also verify claims on independent fact-checking websites.[8] If the theory is not supported by these fact-checking websites, it is more likely to be a conspiracy theory. Next, a reader can note the tone of the theory to discern whether it is a conspiracy theory.[8] Mostly, conspiracy theorists present their information in a way that makes it appear to be the only valid truth. They raise questions rather than provide answers and demonise whoever they think is behind the hypothesized secret plot. Moreover, they present highly subjective and emotionally charged arguments with little to no evidence.[8] They may also use emotional images or anecdotes to prove their point. On the other hand, authors of actual theories are more likely to explore and critically evaluate their point of view. They do not hesitate to include different points of view and acknowledge limits to their knowledge. They include objective and factual evidence.

There is significant hesitancy regarding the study of conspiracy theories in academia. Scholars are often afraid of aligning their studies with controversial topics and therefore, avoid examining and investigating conspiracies.[9] This can have detrimental effects, as avoiding these topics only strengthen the arguments of conspiracy theorists. While the existence of conspiracy theories should fuel more research on the topic, often the mandates of institutions and grant organizations draw focus to other subjects. However, not all conspiracy theories are unfounded and some may even have positive consequences. Conspiracies are a way for people to question actions or decisions taken by authorities.[2,16] This can also lead to greater transparency as authorities want to avoid misconceptions. Additionally, conspiracies surrounding historical events can uncover new information.[17] An example of this is the case of project MKUltra. MK-Ultra, was the name given to a secret project undertaken by the United States Central Intelligence Agency (CIA).[20] This project conducted illegal experiments on human subjects some of which included using drugs such as LSD to weaken targets and brainwash them into confessing crimes. Multiple experiments were also conducted on Canadians using techniques such as hypnosis, sensory deprivation, isolation etc. What started out as genuine curiosity among people about the CIA's work uncovered information on such horrific experimentation.

On the other hand, exposure to conspiracies can also have detrimental effects. For example, exposure to anti-vaccine conspiracies can decrease the likelihood of people getting vaccines and compromising their health. Moreover, exposure to anti-climate or anti-government conspiracies can negatively influence views on politics and climate change. For example, people exposed to the "climate change is a hoax" conspiracy may not believe activists and their pleas for change which are backed up by data. It can be challenging to differentiate between conspiracy theories and factual information. Readers should be encouraged to engage in critical thinking, questioning and fact-checking.[12] People should be warned against the existence of such theories and asked to look into the evidence the theorists provide. Next, instead of spreading conspiracy theories, educated readers should actively engage in debunking myths. They should communicate facts and avoid reinforcing such theories.

Conclusion

In order to understand conspiracy theories, it is important to define and categorize them. Conspiracy theories are loosely defined as the hypothesized actions of a group of people that are conducted in secret. These actions are theorized to have a large impact on society, mostly for the worse. While conspiracy theories can have a positive impact, namely increasing transparency and allowing people to question actions and behaviors of authority figures, they can also detrimentally affect society by spreading misinformation. People that believe in conspiracy theories are convinced that they have special access to confidential information. These beliefs can be motivated by fear, misinformation or the need to resolve ambiguity surrounding a topic. Some conspiracy theorists also aim to manipulate other people's opinions by consciously manipulating evidence. Hence, readers should always be careful of the knowledge they seem to support. In order to be more efficient in discriminating between real theories and unfounded conspiracies, readers must engage in rational thinking and fact-check information found on the internet. They should also check sources before blindly accepting the arguments presented. Defining conspiracy theories and understanding how to spot a conspiracy theory is the first step in combating the spread of misinformation.

CHAPTER 3

The consequences of misinformation

Written by Haya Sonawala

Conspiracy theories can be a lot of fun to indulge in. There are countless videos on the internet speculating about untold truths behind major historical events. These speculations are enjoyable to talk and think about, whether it be with friends in hushed voices as if telling ghost stories or on the internet with the intention of creating just enough doubt to get a certain number of likes and comments. At first, the consequences of these theories may not seem dire, in fact, they're taken more as a joke than anything else. People enjoy jesting about fake news, particularly since the popularization of the term after the 2016 US presidential election,[1] and teasing flat earthers—afterall, they don't cause much harm besides perhaps convincing others that the earth truly is flat, despite that idea being disproved. However, the misinformation and doubt created and spread by conspiracy theories can have adverse consequences that can lead to unforeseen damage. This chapter will break down the consequences of misinformation into three sections: social, ethical, and historical; each section will discuss the risk of conspiracy theories, as well as case studies of specific conspiracies that have caused immeasurable damage.

Social Consequences

Biases can be a common consequence of conspiracy theories. These theories are built on assumptions, and making certain leaps in judgement, and with these assumptions comes prejudice. Biases can take many forms whose consequences have been dire throughout history. A bias is defined as an unjust prejudice in favour of or against a person or a group of people.[2] While such beliefs may be inherited or impressed through a multitude of avenues, the media is a common medium through which biases and prejudice is spread. A journalist who has a certain set of beliefs has a platform to share them, and while they may do this intentionally, though that would break the guidelines of journalistic ethics, they may do this unintentionally, which can be even more dangerous. It is the responsibility of a journalist to share factual information, as this is what the public relies on them for, and through their position they have a significant degree of influence on the masses. Most of the population that watches the news accepts the presented conclusions, which not only means that they become complicit in the biases of journalists, but also that the conclusions may act as the seed for further prejudice as well as actions that may stem from that prejudice.

Biases are especially dangerous in media and journalism because many people consider the news a trusted source of information, and accept the conclusions it presents. However, in recent years, around the time of the 2016 election, the idea of fake news was popularized. The definitions of the term "fake news" can vary drastically. Berkowitz and Schwartz suggest that fake news is news that "blurs the line between nonfiction".[3] However, this poses the question: what is fiction? The term can be difficult to define in journalism; do biases immediately make a journalistic piece fiction, because it is no longer objectively factual? In order to further clarify the term, Bakir and McStay[4] turn to an article written by Wardle,[5] who breaks the term into seven categories: satire or parody, false connection, misleading content, false context, imposter content, manipulated content, and fabricated content. Fake news can be considered both a cause and a consequence of conspiracy theories; a consequence due to the fact that individuals who believe in conspiracy theories might write fake news— whether it be justified through confirmation bias or belong in Wardle's manipulated content category—and a cause because we begin "assessing social and democratic problems with contemporary fake news",[4] and in doing so further solidify our own misconceptions.

Biases and prejudice have manifested themselves in the form of notable movements in history, such as the Salem Witch Trials, and also more recently with the backlash and hate crimes towards Muslims in the post 9/11 world, and a rise of East Asian hate after the start of the COVID-19 pandemic. The media has had a strong role in both of these recent cases— journalists develop their own biases and, whether or not they do this intentionally, they use their large platform to spread this misinformation.

9/11: How Biases Harm Minority Communities

9/11 was a devastating tragedy for an entire nation. It continues to impact those who lost loved ones, those who survived, those who witnessed it live and were traumatized, and for the Muslim community in the West, who are still labelled as terrorists and continue to be the victims of hate crimes.

After the attacks, "some who were unable to cope with the devastation and the failure to prevent them turned to alternative explanations as to how and why these attacks occurred",[6] these explanations being, of course, conspiracy theories. Alexander Riley states that conspiracy theories focus "on a dynamic of us and them".[7] Muslims have been at the centre of the narrative surrounding the attack since the beginning, but the narrative has been far from accurate. Riley addresses different conspiracy theories that arose from both the right and the left of the political spectrum; from the right, the theory is that the memorial for those lost in the attack was "an Islamist plot designed to denigrate the victims and venerate Islamist terrorism".[7] Muslims had not been a prominent part of American history before this event, and as a result the exponentially popular negative narrative surrounding Islamic communities further emphasized the 'us' and 'them' mentality that Riley discussed. The issue with this mentality, particularly when aligned with the sudden and unprecedented coverage of Islam in the media, and especially after a tragedy is that it creates large amounts of animosity. This translates into biases and prejudice, which creates a cycle of misinformation and hateful actions. The damage done to the Muslim ommunity through harmful conspiracy theories is not an isolated incident. Such theories have the potential to impact vulnerable people and sever communities around the world.

Ethical Consequences

Some cases of ignorance seem more forgivable than others. When an individual chooses to believe a conspiracy theory in a way that only affects them, it seems natural to support their individual autonomy, regardless of how different, or even objectively wrong their belief might be. However, there are other cases in which one individual's misinformation can harm the environment and the people around them. This can be classified as an ethical consequence, as it causes objective and tangible harm. This type of consequence of misinformation overlaps with the previously discussed social consequences, because the physical and psychological harm endured by minority communities is an ethical issue. That being said, there is still a distinction between the two: while the social consequences focus on different groups of people and the relationship between people, the ethical consequences take a more theoretical approach, in that it is a discussion of right and wrong, and how that might change from person to person.

Responses to COVID-19 Pandemic

A perfect example of an ethical consequence of misinformation is the public response to the COVID-19 pandemic, and the government issued regulations that came with it. Governments all around the world have put in place guidelines for the public to remain safe, the most common ones being to wear a mask and social distance. However, with the rise of COVID-19 came the rise of conspiracy theories regarding the origins and validity of the illness, as well as questioning the government's intentions in administering the guidelines. This issue was only exacerbated by the development of the vaccine.

The conspiracy theories surrounding the COVID-19 vaccine are not new. There have been misconceptions about many and all vaccines in the past, claiming that they cause autism, implants the patient with a tracking chip, makes the patient magnetic, and much more. While anti-vaxxers have been the subject of a lot of criticism in the past, their refusal to believe scientific evidence, instead opting to believe in conspiracy theories, has become much more dire since the beginning of the pandemic. Due to the highly contagious nature of this virus, "controlling the spread of the novel coronavirus COVID-19 requires widescale public adoption of preventative measures".[8] As such, individuals who choose not to wear a mask, social distance, and/or take the vaccine are not only increasing their own chances of contracting the virus but also risking the lives of their loved ones and those they come in contact with.

This issue is not confined to any one country. For example, Pakistan is a very densely populated country, which makes social distancing difficult already, but the spread of misinformation in Pakistan has significantly aggravated this issue. Recently, a widely circulated WhatsApp message has claimed that Luc Montagnier, a Nobel Prize Winner, stated that everyone who has received the vaccine will die in two years, and that there is no hope for anyone once that have received any vaccine.[9] The Assam Police as well as the Press Information Bureau went on social media "to say that WhatsApp forward is fake news", yet the spread of the message has made its impact, and many are now refusing the vaccine because of it. Using Pakistan as the example, the consequences of this conspiracy theory can be seen in their high case count. While many of these cases can be attributed to the country's lack of resources, the hoarding of vaccines by wealthy countries, as well as new variants of the virus constantly surfacing, the high numbers of new cases and new deaths highlight the risk that individuals are taking by indulging in the conspiracy theories and spreading the misinformation.

This is further confirmed by a study done by Daniel Romer and Kathleen Hall Jamieson, in which they explore the effect conspiracy theories have had on people's response to the virus during the pandemic. The results of the study demonstrated that belief in conspiracy theories was "inversely related to the (a) perceived threat of the pandemic, (b) taking of preventative actions, including wearing a face mask, (c) perceived safety of vaccination, and (d) intention to be vaccinated against COVID-19".[8] It is also known that understanding the threat that the pandemic poses and thereby following the preventative guidelines such as wearing a mask, social distancing, and getting the vaccine, will limit the spread of the virus. Therefore, individuals who choose to indulge in these conspiracy theories and act accordingly, although they may believe that they are doing the right thing, are ethically responsible for not only the harm they may be directly causing to those around them by increasing their chances of infection, but also for those whose risk of infection they have increased by spreading the misinformation. The COVID-19 pandemic is not the only case in which one needs to be aware of their ethical responsibility to be correctly informed. In cases such as these, constant and thorough education of the population is dire for a healthy society.

Historical Consequences

The majority of the social and ethical consequences of conspiracy theories seem to affect the present and the near future, without demonstrating much warning of having long term effects. As the consequences of the conspiracies surrounding 9/11 proved, however, conspiracy theories can be destructive to minority communities, because they can easily become targets for the public to displace their anger, frustration, and trauma onto. Given these consequences, is it possible that the way certain minorities are widely perceived today might affect how they are perceived by historians or societies in the future? Further, could that misguided perception lead to more prejudice, biases, conspiracy theories, and ultimately, a repetitive cycle of the previously discussed consequences. Through examining how narratives surrounding past events come to us in the present, the impact of contemporary conspiracies on the future may be better understood.

The Mongol Empire

The Mongol Empire has been victim to the first of the posed questions. The atrocities inflicted by the empire are widely known by the public—everyone knows the name Genghis Khan, and with it they affiliate murder, battles, and an unwittingly large number of progeny.

The Catholic Church has killed over 60 million from the inquisition and the crusades alone, while the Mongols killed about 40 million. We continue to find the remains of atrocities committed by the Church, the hundreds of unmarked graves in Canadian Residential schools that the Pope is yet to apologize for being only one example of many. Yet, the Church is continued to be held in high regard by the general public and Catholic schools continue to be common in many countries. While there is no reason for these things to cease operation, given of course that the Church's actions reflect how the institution is perceived, it does highlight the injustice history has done against the Mongols.

Because of the narrative surrounding the Mongol Empire, many of their positive achievements and contributions to modern society have been overlooked. Despite using violence to expand their empire, their expansion politically unified the entirety of Eurasia for the first time. In doing this, the empire sparked the beginning of a continuous world history. This is because the unified area created an increase in the trading of goods and knowledge. The Mongols created a welcoming environment for traders by overlooking and accepting cultural differences, in doing so, they were able to overcome the traditional limitations of trade at the time. This also paved the way for the incorporation of various cultures, and the Mongols did this without forcing their own habits and customs onto these other cultures. The Mongols were also the first empire to create a macro economy with multiple centres of production.[10]

Yet, all of this is overlooked by today's general public in favour of the narrative that the Mongols were nothing but ruthless killers and conquerors. It puts into perspective how seemingly harmless contemporary conspiracy theories and misinformation might present us to societies in the future, and perhaps further create misinformation.

While conspiracy theories may be fun, they should be approached with a grain of salt. It would be advisable to critically think through and research stories and theories that are being circulated, rather than accept every piece of information found on the Internet. Understanding journalistic biases as well as one's own biases while researching is vital to an accurate understanding of conspiracy theories, and how they might harm our society.

CHAPTER 4

Why people believe: existential motives

Written by Khushi Shah

In order to understand why people believe in existential motives, it is important to first recognize what existential motives are in the first place. Based on psychology, existential motives are about the focused beliefs that the essence of humankind is their existence, and they can further be explained through the concept of conspiracy theories.[2] Existential motives differ from epistemic and social motivations insofar as existential motives refer to the desire of an individual to be in control of their environment, while epistemic and social motives refer to an understanding of the environment and the desire to maintain a positive social reputation, respectively.[2] Moreover, researchers in the field of psychology and psychotherapy explain that existential psychology is the understanding of the concept that what makes a person whole has multiple factors. These factors include observing an individual's interpersonal relationships, understanding the multiple levels of self-awareness in both an abstract and non-abstract context, examining an individual's free will and what they do with it as they are participants in a experiment not observers of such in their own lives, and understanding how people have different life purposes, values, and meanings.[2] Therapists who treat their patients and practice existential psychology, as a result, treat their patients by stepping into their shoes, essentially submerging themselves in the patient's world. These therapists practice treating their patients in order to find the meaning of the person's existence and understanding the patient's whole personal history.[2]

Then it comes to question how the concept of where existential psychology originates and what factors influence its inception. The subject draws heavily from the works of Soren Kierkegaard, who was a Danish philosopher during the 1800s.[3] Soren Kierkegaard is commonly referred to as the "The Father of Existentialism," as he was the first person to introduce the idea that "I exist, therefore I think".[3] The subject draws heavily from the works of philosopher Rene Descarte's statement "I think, therefore I am".[3] This simple change of one word from "am" to "think" caused an uproar within the European philosophical and psychological communities at the time, and while the statement was controversial at first, it would go on to influence a new approach to philosophical and psychological analysis.[3] While gaining traction in Europe, Soren Kierkegaard's existential philosophy was not readily accepted in the United States of America. Rollo May was an American psychologist who was a strong supporter of Kierkegaard's work and existential psychology as a wholet.3 During the 1950s, Rollo May and psychologist philosopher William James successfully brought existential psychology to the US, as they had collectively framed the existential motives concept of psychology in an American context.[3] Rollo May initially found out about the concept of existential motives from Paul Tillich in New York, who was studying to be a Congregationalist minister from the Union Theological Seminary. William James brought discussions of free will to the existentialist context, which is now an essential component of the existential thought process.[3] Existential psychology began being introduced to students in university classrooms during the 1920s and 1930s.[3] One of the first university professors to champion the idea of existential psychology in his classroom as well as his research was Viktor Frankl.[3] Frankl stated that he was very intrigued bythe ideas brought forward by existential psychology based on his experiences during WWII where he was imprisoned in Theresienstadt, a Nazi death camp. Thus, Frankl wrote that his ideas were deeply influenced by how he felt and viewed the world due to the trauma he had experienced.[3] Existential psychology as a discipline would be officially introduced to the greater subject of psychological motives on September 5, 1959.[3] This was the date when psychologists Rollo May, Abraham Maslow, and Herman Feifel presented at the American Psychological Association (APA) Symposium on Existential Psychology and Psychotherapy with the goal of reaching a larger audience of professionals in order to change the trajectory of psychological thought and practice.[3] Post the American Psychological Association Symposium in the 1960s, the concept of existentialism became a "buzz" word in the world of psychology. Rollo May described the existential approach to psychotherapy and treatment of patients as the main task of therapy now becomes understanding the patient as a whole, looking at the patient in one's own shoes and understanding their entire existence.[3] This form of therapy would also require the patients to commit to the understanding of existential psychotherapy, where they would be required to fully describe to the therapist and/or professional the lives they were living vs the lives in which they were existing.

Furthermore, existentialism gained popularity during World War II and made a big impact on the baby boomer generation especially, as this form of psychology had fully taken root by the 1960's when members of this generation were reaching adulthood.[3] This is due to existentialism being accepted in people's daily lives, instead of only being talked about and taught in universities and privately by psychologists and philosophers. An example of how the idea of existential motives became common in people's daily lives is that Rollo May came out with a novel called "Love and Will" which explained to people the new age of existential psychology and the meaning behind this way of thinking.[3] This book stayed on the United States of America's bestseller lists for over half a year, it's popularity owing in part to the fact that the book was written for individuals of various educational backgrounds, allowing for the book to impact the general population for decades.[3] Moreover, existentialism was also introduced to wider audiences through self-help and self-improvement novels, which started to incorporate it into their advice, encouraging individuals to explore deeply within their own existence.

People believe in existential motives because of our need as humans to feel safe and secure in our environment. Moreover, individuals enjoy being able to exert control over the environment they reside in, presenting themselves as autonomous individuals and members of collectives. Believing in conspiracy theories allows people to have compensatory satisfaction with how the world works and how they fit into it. As a result, individuals turn to conspiracy theories based on existential psychology in order to deal with the feeling that their needs are not being threatened, by acquiring a greater understanding of the world.[1] For example, individuals who lack control in their lives or who feel threatened by the lack of instrumental control have been proven to feel some compensatory sense of control by the concept of conspiracy theories.[1] These individuals feel this way because it allows them the opportunity to disregard any official narratives that make them feel out of control. Conspiracy theories additionally make people feel safer as they present a form of cheater detection.[1] Cheater detection is when dangerous and/or untrustworthy individuals are identified as threats and can therefore be eliminated or reduced1. Research studies exhibit the fact that individuals get further motivated to lean towards conspiracy theories when they feel anxious or lack self-control and power. An example of this in the present day is the multiple conspiracy theories that come out regarding COVID-19 and 9/11 where people feel unsafe in their own environments, and thus turn to these theories to provide them with some sense of closure or explanation for what is happening around them. Another research study states that those who believe in conspiracy theories have been linked to also have a strong relationship to a lack of sociopolitical control and a lack of psychological empowerment, as they evidently feel not in control of their decisions based on themselves and the world around them (specifically linked to politics and voting).[1] Further experiments show that in comparison to normal baseline conditions, the motivation to believe in conspiracy theories is heightened when individuals feel an inability to control their outcomes and is reduced when they feel like their sense of control is regained. Although many research studies explain existential psychology in correlation to conspiracy theories, no research done thus far indicates that conspiracy theories do not make individuals feel one hundred percent secure, although they do seem to help.[1] Moreover, participants in conspiracy theory experiments have been observed to almost immediately lose and/or suppress their sense of autonomy and control as soon as they are introduced to them.[1] As a result, researchers concluded that the motivation to believe in conspiracy theories makes individuals less inclined to make decisions that will inhibit their autonomy and control of themselves in the future.[1] This includes being less inclined to commit to an organization and/or another person, and less likely to engage in political actions such as voting and following along with different parties' policies.[1] A study conducted in 2008 by Douglas and Sutton further stated that individuals believed in the conspiracy theory materials, even though they were not aware that they may have been falsely persuaded to believe in such due to existential psychology and they were unaware that their beliefs before the being exposed to conspiracy theories have been altered as a result.[1] Overall, the existential psychology behind conspiracy theories makes people feel secure. It was also found that they are in the hands of malevolent forces who exercise and possess control beyond the normal limits, thus further research studies are predicted to state that the effect of conspiracy theories is disempowering.

The main goal of existential psychology in terms of therapy is to reduce the distress associated with symptoms of mental health conditions such as anxiety, depression, rage, among others.[2] As a result, this form of therapy is concerned with deeply experiencing and exploring the different symptoms the patient is experiencing as well as directly allowing the symptoms to occur without any suppression or eradication.while this may be seen as an issue by some, is essential to the therapeutic ethos of existential psychology.[2] Existential psychology may be viewed as more exploratory, rather than behaviour and goal-oriented. This is due to the fact that the goal of existential psychology is to clarify, comprehend, describe, and explore one's self as opposed to analyzing, explaining, treating, and/or curing someone's subjective experience of suffering. To this end, existential therapists use the skills of empathic reflection, Socratic questioning, and active listening. Some techniques are tweaked versions of different therapeutic approaches which include psychoanalysis, cognitive behavioural therapy, person-centred, and the Gestalt form of therapy.[2] Existential therapy provides a great deal of flexibility, as the professionals are able to tailor particular responses or interventions in order to suit the unique needs of the patient at hand.

Existential psychology and existential motives center around the belief that the essence of humankind is their existence, and that wellbeing stems from being safe, having a total understanding, and being in control of an individual's environment. The main reason why individuals turn to existential motives is due to the need for humankind to feel safe and secure in their own environment. An area where existential motives directly apply is the concept of conspiracy theories, with people's belief in conspiracy theories allowing them to have compensatory satisfaction in how the world works and how they fit into it. Individuals who lack control in their lives or feel threatened by the lack of instrumental control have been proven to feel some compensatory sense of control by the concept of conspiracy theories. Research demonstrates that in comparison to normal baseline conditions, the motivation to believe in conspiracy theories is heightened when individuals feel an inability to control the outcomes of their environment, and is reduced when they feel like their sense of control is regained.[2] Furthermore, the main goal of existential therapy is to tone down distress and the symptoms of mental health conditions though redirecting and understanding those feelings to help individuals regain a sense of control. Examples of such include mental health conditions such as anxiety, depression, rage, and etcetera; through the means of empathic reflection, Socratic questioning, active listening, psychoanalysis, cognitive behavioural therapy, person-centred, and the Gestalt form of therapy. Overall, the concept of existential psychology is very broad, but it has proven to be helpful to individuals as it is a prominent aspect of the world today and will continue to be researched/explored further.

CHAPTER 5

Why people believe: social motives

Written by Iqra Abid

Introduction to Social Motives

Unsurprisingly, conspiracy theories have a largely social component. They are also much more common than the general public would believe. This is because conspiracy theories are the result of everyday cognitive processes, meaning anyone can believe in conspiracies.[2] A social psychologist perspective uncovers some of these mechanisms, including sense-making, defining group membership, perspective-taking, projection, and pattern perception.[2] Such processes explain the role that social identity and intergroup relationships have on an individual's belief in conspiracy theories. This chapter explores how self-image and social identity shape intergroup perceptions, the psychological mechanisms that aid these perceptions, and how conspiracy theories often rely on intergroup conflict. The social motivations of conspiracy theories rely on self-image and intergroup conflict.

Self-Image

The self is a reflective state of conscious thought and feelings acquired through experience.[4] It is formed by understanding the self relative to other things in the world (people, objects, environment, etc.). Self-image refers to the subjective perception of our own self and it is subject to change in social situations.[4] Social interactions and social environments often change the way we think and feel, even temporarily. Despite its extensive impact on our everyday lives, people are typically unaware of this effect on self-image.[4]

Social situations affect self-image because of our tendency to make social comparisons. Social comparisons have the ability to make us feel bad or good, and they shape our own perceptions and identity.[4] For example, one study had first and fourth year undergraduate students read a story regarding a former student's success.[1] The students were then asked to rate their self-worth after reading the story. First year students experienced higher self-esteem because they felt motivated, meanwhile, fourth year students experienced lowered self-esteem because they felt the former's student's accomplishments were unattainable.[1] A control group of first and fourth year students didn't receive a story to read and expressed equal and average self-esteem.[1] This study illustrates how social comparisons occur through social interactions and demonstrates the effect that social comparisons have on self-esteem and thus, self-image. Social comparisons play an important role in forming identities, impacting what groups people identify with.

A central social motive for conspiracy theorizing is the desire to maintain a positive image of the self or group.[1, 3, 5] Poor self-image and low self-esteem have negative effects on life outcomes. It is also just a negative experience that humans have an innate response to avoid.[4] This results in phenomena like cognitive dissonance, the uncomfortable tension of saying or doing something you do not morally agree with, and cognitive biases like the fundamental attribution error, the tendency to justify your own behaviours with external factors while explaining the behaviours of others as if they are inherently flawed. Generally, people unconsciously avoid harming their self-esteem at all costs.[4] This is where conspiracy theories help as they can boost or uphold self-image and sense of positive group affiliations which is typically achieved by blaming negative outcomes on others.[1] By avoiding blame and negative associations, people are able to preserve their self-image.

Sense-making, the desire to make sense of the world and one's role in it, can make people more susceptible to conspiracy theories. When sense-making tendencies lead to belief in conspiracy theories, it can be a result of poor self-image and social interactions. For instance, research shows that social exclusion leads people to turn to such theories to make sense of negative social experiences and a lack of connection to social groups.[1] In this case, the social need to belong is not being met, causing people to feel disadvantaged or disenfranchised by society and leading to low self-image. Those who are socially isolated then try to make sense of their feelings and experiences using conspiracy theories.

Conspiracy theories are also appealing to narcissists who are people with an inflated sense of self-worth due to underlying insecurities. Narcissists can be drawn to conspiracy theories to fulfill their need to be unique.[2, 3] Researchers argue that conspiracy theories make people feel as if they possess rare and important information that others do not have access to.[1] This makes people feel unique, boosting their self-image as a result. Another social motive includes projection, a social psychological process of projecting traits, motives or behaviours onto others to avoid acknowledging them in oneself.[2] When an observer does not have reliable or objective information, they rely on what they know about themselves; this affects how people make judgements of others regarding their thoughts, feelings and behaviour.[2] As a sense-making mechanism in understanding others, projection can be influenced by low self-image as people unconsciously use their own experiences and behaviours to make judgements of others.[2] When forming conspiracies through projection, the conspiracies arise from unconscious conflicts and purposes.

Social Identity

Identity is a set of integrated ideas about the self, the roles we play based on societal norms and values, and the qualities that make us unique.[4] People define themselves relative to others, specifically other social groups.[4] Group affiliations have become an extension of people's social identity and when the image of a social group suffers, so does the self-image of the individual group members. Forming definitions of groups and perspective-taking are important processes that determine how we navigate and make sense of the world. These socio-cognitive processes have been linked to belief in conspiracy theories.

The role of group membership in the belief of conspiracy theories is a significant one. Parts of social identities are formed by designating social groups as in-groups or out-groups.[6] For example, a White person's in-group consists of other White people and out-groups would consist of other racial groups. People identify with in-groups on the basis of their connection to the group.[6] If someone did not like rock music, their in-group would not be fans of rock music, thus creating an out-group of rock music fans. Since social identities are partially made up of the social groups people identify with, group affiliations have the power to impact one's self-image. This means that people also want to uphold the image of their in-group(s) to preserve their own self-image.

As a result of forming in-groups and out-groups, people have a tendency to view the social world as "us" versus "them".[6] This is the act of defining social groups and recognizing which group one belongs to. Once formed, these group affiliations become a part of one's social identity.[5] The social groups that are identified with become a person's community, determine their social environments, and more often than not, their beliefs are also shaped by the beliefs held by other group members. When the "us" is victimized, people become concerned.

The stronger someone is connected to their group identity, the more likely it is that they will believe a conspiracy theory when that group becomes victimized.[5, 6] This is where perspective-taking plays a role. Perspective-taking is a method of trying to understand a situation from someone else's perspective to invoke feelings of empathy and a stronger identification to the other person.[6] Perspective-taking can be a pro-social behaviour, improving relationships between groups to reduce stereotyping and prejudice.[6] As a pro-social behaviour, it helps groups care for other social groups and behave in the interest of their collective good instead of self-interest. It reduces and does not enforce negative perceptions of out-groups.[6] Perspective-taking with conspiracies creates a stronger connection to the portrayed victims of a conspiracy. It also stimulates motivation to understand and make sense of the event.[6] Perspective-taking and our sense-making tendencies increase the likelihood that a person will believe a conspiracy theory in which the victims belong to their own social group.

Intergroup Conflict

Perspective-taking can also be dangerous as strong connections to a social group can foster a sense of superiority compared to other groups, leading to intergroup conflict.[6] This manifests as collective narcissism, an exaggerated belief in the superiority of one's in-group accompanied by the need for external validation.[3] The need for external validation is a product of the sense of superiority and the belief that their in-group is undervalued, underprivileged or under threat. Due to collective narcissism, people will perceive all other groups as inferior, even morally inferior, allowing them to believe other groups are conspiring against their own.[3] People who do not experience collective narcissism have a lower likelihood of believing in conspiracies,[3] while the more narcissistic someone is about their group, the more likely they are to believe other groups are conspiring against them.[1] As such, conspiracy theorizing is typically due to the need for external validation at the expense of disparaging out-groups.

This belief that an in-group is being targeted due to its superiority is referred to as out-group threat where out-groups are perceived to be powerful, untrustworthy, and capable of harm.[6] out-group threat is a common social motivator for believing in conspiracy theories. For instance, Anti-Semitic conspiracy theories are created with the belief that all Jewish people are inferior and are motivated to harm non-Jewish people.[1, 6] These kinds of conspiracy theories have the power to harbour and enforce hatred, prejudice and discrimination against different social groups, creating intergroup conflict.[8] Conspiracy theories help paint the image of one's in-groups in a positive light while framing other groups as a powerful but immoral force.[6]

Conspiracy theories involving out-group threats usually form when societal systems and the social status quo are being questioned.[6, 8] People who have their needs met by the current societal system are more likely to form or believe in conspiracy theories as a defensive response to those challenging the system.[6] When the societal system is perceived to be threatened, the groups that like the way system functions feel as if their needs are at risk. This makes them more susceptible to conspiracy theories that justify the need for the system to exist.[8] These conspiracies identify one or more out-groups and blame them for all social ills, framing them as conspirers.[6] In blaming an out-group for the negative aspects of the system, conspiracy theories assert that only the conspiring group is at fault for all of society's ills and the system is functioning as it was intended to.[6] This enforces prejudiced thinking, forming and upholding stereotypes of other social groups, and oftentimes leads to discrimintaion. People are also drawn to conspiracy theories because they reflect and validate their preexisting beliefs against other social groups.[5] In this sense, conspiracy theories play a significant role in enforcing and contributing to intergroup conflict.

Conspiracies are often formed during societal crises and situational threats, usually centring socio-political events, for multiple reasons.[1, 3] These crises and events are periods of rapid and impactful social change that tend to question societal systems and the social status quo. Social groups who feel comfortable and have their needs met by the system begin to feel as if their group is under threat because of those challenging the system. Archival data reveals that powerless people of the past have used conspiracy theories to defend themselves during major socio-political events, suggesting that people on the losing side of politics are more likely to believe in conspiracies.[1] These crises and threatening situations also invoke feelings of powerlessness, uncertainty and a loss of control.[3, 8] Feelings of uncertainty and threat make people more open to conspiracy theorizing as they try to make sense of the situation and their own position in it.[6, 7] An example of sense-making is pattern perception where people seek to assign meaning to random socio-political events by perceiving patterns and connections that do not exist.[2] Actively looking for patterns increases pattern perception tendencies, a behaviour that predicts belief in conspiracies.[2]

Times of crisis strengthen group attachments and as explained earlier, a stronger connection to a social identity or group increases the likelihood of fostering conspiracy beliefs. It is important to note that this increased attachment only occurs when the event or situation is relevant to the theorist in some way.[6] This means that conspiracy theorists do not believe in every conspiracy, they only believe those with victims they are able to connect to or identify with.[6] This combination of uncertainty, threat, and stronger group attachment leads to increased susceptibility to conspiracy theories. These conspiracies often frame other social groups as the cause of all of society's ills, fostering and enforcing prejudice and discrimination against other groups. Conspiracy theories are essentially characterized by intergroup conflict through the perception of other social groups in comparison to one's own groups. Collective narcissism, out-group threat and socio-political events or crises are all social factors that motivate belief in conspiracy theories.

Minority Groups

When it comes to minority groups, their belief in conspiracy theories are typically shaped by the need to belong, as well as situational and crisis threats. For minority groups, the need to belong is different as minority groups have a strong sense of in-group identity.[6] The need to belong occurs on a larger societal scale as minority groups have been excluded from or discriminated against by most parts of the societal system and more powerful majority groups.[1] Again, feeling disadvantaged plays a central role in this explanation. For example, research has found that Black Americans were more likely to believe conspiracy theories in which the American government was conspiring against the Black population than White Americans.[1] Furthermore, people are more likely to believe in conspiracies directed at their own group when they have personally experienced discrimination.[1]

The belief in conspiracy theories by minority group members is a response to threats and inequalities rooted in reality and is a result of histories filled with threat and victimization.[1] As such, situational and crisis threats like discrimination and events challenging the societal systems and social status quo, play an important role in minority group members' susceptibility to conspiracy theories. For this reason, it is important to consider the socio-political and historical contexts that make conspiracy theories so believable to minority group members. Situational and crisis threats are also causes for increased group attachment which predicts belief in conspiracy theories. As a result, societal exclusion and crisis threats allow minority group members to believe in conspiracy theories more strongly; however, research indicates belief of conspiracy theories is not as common in minority groups as it is in other groups.[8] While more research must be conducted regarding conspiracy beliefs among minority groups, this suggests that the largest social motivators are collective narcissism and intergroup conflict among majority groups.[1, 8]

Conclusion

To summarize, the central social motivators of conspiracy theories are self-image, social identity and the intergroup conflict that arises from social identity formation. Many socio-cognitive mechanisms play a role in the appeal of conspiracy theories including: sense-making, the need to understand the world and oneself; defining group memberships to determine what groups you connect to; perspective-taking— the ability to perceive someone else's point of view to invoke feelings of empathy; projection— the social process of unconsciously assigning your own motives, attitudes, and behaviours to others to preserve self-esteem; and pattern perception— the practice of seeking patterns that leads one to believe patterns exist where they do not. These mechanisms also explain phenomena like collective narcissism, an exaggerated sense of superiority of one's group compared to others, and out-group threat, the belief that an out-group is conspiring against your own group. The need to feel unique is also a social motivator, typically for narcissists, leading people to believe in conspiracy theories because they feel they have special information and this feeling compensates for underlying insecurities while feeding an exaggerated sense of self-importance.

Essentially, people believe in conspiracy theories to boost their own self-image by protecting the image of their in-group. Since group affiliations are socialized into parts of our identities, negative group images place people's self-image at risk. To protect their self-image, people become more open to conspiracy theories that positively portray their in-group.

In threatening situations or socio-political crises, uncertainty and loss of control strengthens people's connections to their in-group and inspires a need to understand the situation and their position. These feelings combined with these sense-making tendencies increases the likelihood that people will believe in conspiracy theories with victims they can identify with, especially if they have experienced discrimination before. Thus, conspiracy theorizing is highest when people need to feel better about themselves and their social groups, and when people need to make sense of their environment to feel safe and in control.

CHAPTER 6

Breaking down specific theories and their origins

Written by Anna Yang

Introduction

Conspiracy theories run rampant in modern day society, fuelled by the rise of social media over the past decade. According to Cynthia Miller-Idriss, an American University sociology professor who specializes in extremism and radicalization, people tend to turn to conspiracy theories when they feel out of control, afraid, and anxious.[1] Conspiracy theories offer comfort in the form of a black and white answer while simultaneously shielding people from having to fully face and comprehend the shocking events occurring in reality.[1] As such, it comes with little surprise that some of the most shocking events in human history, such as the Apollo 11 moon landings, 9/11 attacks, and COVID-19 pandemic have been accompanied by a multitude of conspiracy theories. In this chapter, prominent conspiracy theories such as the moon landing conspiracy, conspiracy theories regarding 9/11, the flat earth conspiracy theory, and various conspiracy theories surrounding COVID-19 will be explored.

The Moon Landing Conspiracy Theory

There is an extraordinary amount of evidence that Apollo 11 astronauts Neil Armstrong and Buzz Aldrin did indeed land on the lunar surface on July 20, 1969, and that the subsequent Apollo moon landings were authentic as well. This vast body of evidence includes the 382 kilograms of moon rock collected across the six missions, our ability to bounce laser beams off the gear left on the moon by the astronauts, images of the Apollo landing sites and the tracks made by the astronauts in the moondust taken by NASA's Lunar Reconnaissance Orbiter, and corroboration from Russia, Japan, and China.[2] Despite this, belief in the conspiracy theory that the Apollo moon landings were faked have thrived since 1969 and persist today, with opinion polls in recent years consistently showing that around 5% of Americans believe that the Apollo moon landings were faked.[3]

Doubts that the moon landings were technologically possible are hardly novel phenomena; they are as old as the moon landings themselves, with jokes about faked moon landings emerging as early as 1971, in the James Bond movie "Diamonds Are Forever."[3] However, the first instance in which the topic was treated with serious consideration was in 1976, when Bill Kaysing self-published a book titled We Never Went to the Moon: America's Thirty Billion Dollar Swindle, in which he argued that the American government faked the moon landing and filmed it in a studio in Area 51 as a way of triumphing over the Soviets in the Space Race.[4] Kaysing's alleged claim to expertise was that he had worked briefly as a technical writer at Rocketdyne, a company that helped design the Saturn V rocket engines.[2] He claimed that this job had given him access to documents proving that the Apollo mission was a hoax.[5] The primary basis for Kaysing's argument was the fact that stars are not visible in the photos of the Apollo 11 landing.[4] Many have since remarked that the most likely explanation for this is that the camera's aperture was not wide enough to capture the light from the stars.[4] However, in the times in which Kaysing published his book, which happened to be situated in the wake of Watergate, the Vietnam War, and the release of the details of the MKUltra, a CIA mind control project, the American public was fully primed to be skeptical of their government.[4] As such, the ideal circumstances existed for Kaysing's ideas to take root and grow. In fact, according to a Gallup poll from 1976, during this time, nearly 28% of Americans believed the moon landing was faked.[4]

Kaysing's conspiracy theory was further propelled into popular culture by the release of the film "Capricorn One" in 1978.[4] This Peter Hyams film tells the story of a journalist who uncovers a government hoax involving a faked Mars landing.[4] This film, although fictional and not directly linked to the moon, did much to promote the idea that the moon landing was staged and catapulted the conspiracy theory into the consciousness of the general public. The moon landing conspiracy theory subsequently entered the modern era in 2001, when Fox News broadcast a documentary titled Conspiracy Theory: Did We Land on the Moon?[2] Hosted by the X-Files actor Mitch Pileggi, the documentary essentially repackaged Kaysing's original arguments for consumption by a new audience.[2] Those who worked at NASA at the time recalled a lot of frustration emerging in response to the documentary. As Roger Launius, a former chief historian at NASA has said, "for many years, we refused to respond to this stuff. It wasn't worth giving it a hearing. But when Fox News aired that so-called documentary – stating unequivocally 'we haven't landed on the moon' - it really raised the level. We began to receive all kinds of questions."[2] Since then, other forms of media have contributed to the revitalization of the moon landing conspiracy theories in modern times. The television show "The X-Files," for instance, brought all sorts of space conspiracy theories into the public consciousness in the 1990s and 2000s, and the reboot addressed the moon landing in an episode in 2018.[3] The popular Youtuber Shane Dawson, who has more than 22 million subscribers, also contributed to this revitalization by promoting the idea that the moon landing was faked in one of his videos.[4] Although he did not explicitly say that he believes that NASA faked the moon landing, he did say that it would not be a shock, with his exact words being: "Why wouldn't the moon landing be fake? Why wouldn't we fake that, just to win over other countries? It makes you wonder, have we actually ever been to the moon?"[4]

Despite the popularity of this conspiracy theory, the large community of supporters that has grown around the notion of a faked moon landing has failed to produce any significant evidence in favour of their theory. The theory itself is primarily baseless conjecture, while the limited pieces of evidence offered by supporters have been firmly refuted by scientists over the years. The story believed by the majority of moon landing deniers is that the staged moon landing was directed by Stanley Kubrick, who was recruited by NASA for the job following his work on the 1968 movie "2001: A Space Odyssey."[4] Kubrick purportedly spent 18 months on a soundstage shooting the footage for the Apollo 11 and 12 missions.[4] According to this theory, Kubrick's 1980 film "The Shining" was an apology for his role in deceiving the American public – the basis for this particular portion of the conspiracy theory seems to be that the character Danny Torrance wears an Apollo 11 sweater at one point in the film.[4] Needless to say, this theory itself has little supporting evidence; instead, the moon landing conspiracy is primarily fuelled by the alleged existence of evidence that contradicts the notion that the moon landings were authentic. For instance, the lack of a blast crater under the landing module and the ways in which shadows fall in photos have both been touted as evidence that the moon landings were filmed in a TV studio.[2] Both ideas have been disproved, however, and are due to, respectively, the way thrust works in a vacuum and the reflective qualities of moondust.[2] The common belief that the Van Allen radiation belts would kill any astronauts before they reached the moon does not fare any better, as scientists have pointed out that this is not the case given that the spaceships only move through the radiation belts for a few hours, as opposed to the multiple days that would be necessary for exposure to be fatal.[5] Although the consequences of this conspiracy theory are not as significant as those of theories surrounding more salient issues such as the COVID-19 pandemic or climate change, belief in the moon landing conspiracy can still have negative societal effects such as reducing institutional trust and support for space exploration initiatives.

9/11 Conspiracy Theories

Jamie Gorelick, a member of the 9/11 Commission, knows how persistent conspiracy theories can be once they take root. This was part of the reason that the 9/11 Commission's 2004 report on the September 11, 2001 attacks were written with such rigor, narrative power, and empirical clarity. However, despite the Commission's best efforts to deflate the conspiracy theories surrounding the 9/11 attacks – which began to surface in Internet chat rooms within a few hours of the attacks themselves – these theories were able to grow and still persist to this day.

The 9/11 conspiracy theories began as attacks against President George W. Bush, taking the form of assertions that the Bush administration was concealing the truth behind Al-Qaeda's attacks and doing the bidding of various nefarious forces such as oil companies, the Saudi government, or "the Jews."[6] By 2005, these conspiracy theories were prevalent and prominent enough for the popular science magazine Popular Mechanics to devote an entire special issue to debunking them.[6] Today, a number of theories surrounding the 9/11 attacks remain popular among conspiracy theorists. One of these theories is that the Twin Towers were actually brought down by explosives as opposed to planes. This is one of the most well-known 9/11 conspiracy theories as well as one of the earliest to surface. Believers claim that the collapse of the North and South Towers resembled an act of controlled demolition in the quick rate at which they fell and the fact that they fell into their own footprints.[7] Witness testimonies that report explosions being heard before the Towers collapsed as well as debris being seen shooting from the lower levels of the buildings have also been put forth as evidence.[7] When the official report on the 9/11 attacks stated that the Towers fell due to severe structural damage caused by the planes and resulting fires, conspiracy theorists continued to argue for their viewpoint, claiming that the fires did not burn long enough to cause the collapses.[7]

Another conspiracy theory surrounding the 9/11 attacks is that the Pentagon was struck by a missile as opposed to American Airlines Flight 77.[7] This theory emerged due to the fact that early video footage and photos of the scene did not seem to show evidence of plane wreckage.[7] Conspiracy theorists considered this as evidence that the Pentagon was struck by a missile or unmanned drone instead of a plane.[7] Yet another conspiracy theory claims that United Airlines Flight 93, which crashed into an open field in Pennsylvania after passengers attempted to take it back from the hijackers, was actually shot down by the American military.[7] As with the conspiracy theory surrounding the Pentagon attack, this theory emerged due to the little amount of plane wreckage discovered in the field, which led conspiracy theorists to claim that the crash site was too small for an airliner the size of Flight 93, and that the plane was actually shot down by the American military, causing it to disintegrate over a larger area.[7] Other conspiracy theories involve the notion that various parties within the United States knew of the attacks in advance. For instance, a common belief among conspiracy theorists is that the North American Aerospace Defense Command deliberately ordered their fighter jets to stand down and allow the hijacked planes to reach their targets.[7] The theorists claim that the government wanted to use the attacks to justify an invasion of Iraq and Afghanistan for the sake of securing oil interests.[7] There is no evidence for this theory, and it appears to rest solely on people's disbelief that the United States, which seemingly had the most powerful air force in the world at the time of the attacks, was unable to intercept any of the planes.[7] Belief in 9/11 conspiracy theories has the same consequences that most other conspiracy theories have, such as decreasing institutional support, and also has the additional potential to create social tensions between certain groups due to the long-lasting trauma and emotional impact of the 9/11 attacks.

The Flat Earth Conspiracy Theory

One of the most notorious conspiracy theories of the modern age is the flat earth conspiracy. Believers of the flat earth conspiracy, known as flat earthers, are convinced that the Earth is a flat disc with the Arctic Circle in the centre and Antarctica (believed to be a 150-foot-tall wall of ice) circling the perimeter.[8] These conspiracy theorists formed an organization known as the Flat Earth Society which – in their own words - "mans the guns against oppression of thought and the Globularist lies of a new age. Standing with reason we offer a home to those wayward thinkers that march bravely on with REASON and TRUTH in recognizing the TRUE shape of the Earth – Flat."[9]

The origins of the Flat Earth Society date back to the early 1800s, when the organization was founded by Samuel Birley Rowbotham, an English inventor.[9] Rowbotham's belief in a flat earth was based primarily on literal interpretations of Biblical passages.[9] His model of the solar system, known as Zetetic Astronomy, consisted of the earth as a flat disk with the North Pole at the centre and a wall of ice around the edge, with the sun, moon, and other planets and stars located just a few hundred miles above the earth's surface.[9] Following Rowbotham's death in 1884, his followers founded the Universal Zetetic Society, and from thereon the flat earth theory spread to the United States.[9] The ideas remained relatively unpopular until 1956, when the International Flat Earth Society was formally founded by Samuel Shenton, a Fellow of the Royal Astronomical Society and the Royal Geographic Society.[9] When Shenton died in 1971, Charles K. Johnson succeeded him as the president of the International Flat Earth Society and actively promoted the Society, eventually growing its membership to over 3000.[9] In 1995, however, a fire destroyed the Johnson home, which contained the Flat Earth Society's library, archives, and membership lists.[9] Several years of inactivity followed, until the Flat Earth Society was eventually resurrected in 2004, officially reopening to new members in 2009.[9] Since then, the conspiracy theory has grown in popularity, with the Internet and social media aiding its spread. For instance, in 2015 and 2016, a collection of videos posted by Eric Dubay and Mark Sargent on Youtube re-ignited interest in the flat earth conspiracy, and the existence of the Internet and social media allowed for these ideas to spread with unprecedented ease.[8] A number of people who have investigated the flat earth conspiracy and its believers have noted the significance of the Internet, and Youtube in particular, in fuelling the modern day rise in flat earth beliefs. For instance, Asheley Landrum, a psychologist from Texas Tech University who has attended Flat Earth Conferences for the sake of learning why so many people believe this conspiracy theory, has noted that "almost everybody that [she] spoke to said that either they were directly exposed to flat Earth on Youtube or they were exposed to it via a family member who was exposed to it on Youtube."[10]

Although flat earthers are often referred to as a unified group, it is worth noting that in reality, they are not a singular, cohesive movement. Although all flat earthers share the belief that the earth is flat, there is disagreement among believers regarding the exact nature of the earth's topography. While some believe that the earth is a discreet disc with Antarctica as a wall of ice around the edge, some believe that the earth is instead an infinite plane extending forever in all directions.[8] Other models propose that the flat earth and its atmosphere are encased in a huge, hemispherical snow globe from which nothing can fall off the edges.[10] To account for night and day, most flat earthers believe that the Sun moves in circles around the North Pole, acting as a spotlight.[10] The US model of a flat earth, for instance, suggests that the sun and moon are both 50 kilometres in diameter and circle the flat Earth at a height of 5500 kilometres, with the stars situated above this on a rotating dome.[10] Many flat earthers also reject the notion of gravity, with the UK model of a flat earth asserting that the earth itself is accelerating upwards to give the illusion of gravity.[10]

As is the case with most conspiracy theories, the flat earth conspiracy is driven not by evidence for a flat earth, but by alleged evidence against a round one. As Lee McIntyre, a philosopher from Boston University who specializes in the phenomenon of science denial has remarked, "flat earthers seem to have a very low standard of evidence for what they want to believe but an impossibly high standard of evidence for what they don't want to believe."[10] For instance, photos of distant skylines are often touted by flat earthers as "proof" that the earth is flat. McIntyre, in his interactions with flat earthers, was commonly shown a photo of Chicago, taken from Lake Michigan, in which the city's skyscrapers are visible despite being 100 kilometres away.[10] As those who are more knowledgeable know, the reason that these buildings are visible despite the vast distance is that the air directly above the water's surface is colder than the air higher up in the atmosphere.[10] This temperature gradient means that light rays refract toward the colder and denser air, allowing for an image of the reflected skyline, formed on the water below the horizon, to appear, hovering above the horizon.[10] This explanation is easily verified by taking a photo from a farther distance, which causes the mirage to disappear.[10] With respect to the societal effects of the flat earth conspiracy theory, in addition to decreased institutional trust, there is also the concern that if belief in the theory spreads to those with influence in public education systems, there may be a push to introduce the theory into educational curricula, as has been observed in the past with creationism.

COVID-19 Conspiracy Theories

The most recent genre of conspiracy theories to emerge revolves around the origins of COVID-19. As the virus spread across the world, speculation about its origins did as well. The early days of the pandemic created the perfected conditions for conspiracy theories to emerge and flourish, where an abundance of legitimate questions about COVID-19 existed and knowledge was scarce. One of the most popular COVID-19 conspiracy theories is that the virus is a genetically engineered bioweapon that escaped from a high-level lab in Wuhan, China. This conspiracy theory can be traced back to Francis Boyle, a law professor at the University of Illinois with no academic training in virology or biology.[11] Nonetheless, Boyle is a longstanding critic of research pathogens as well as an experienced conspiracy theorist, having claimed in the past that West Nile virus and Lyme disease both escaped from US biowarfare labs and that Bill Gates was involved in the spread of Zika virus.[11] Boyle first promoted his claim that COVID-19 shows signs of nanotechnological tinkering in an email sent to a list of news organizations and personal contacts on January 24, 2020.[11] That same day, he was interviewed on a podcast called "Geopolitics and Empire" which subsequently went viral, leading to Boyle's comments being featured in Iranian state TV, Russian state media, and fringe websites in the US and around the world.[11] Boyle's theory is based entirely on circumstantial evidence, such as the presence of a Biosafety Level 4 lab in Wuhan, the fact that other viruses have escaped from other labs in the past, as well as his personal, unsubstantiated belief that governments around the world are engaged in a secret biological arms race.[11] None of Boyle's alleged evidence offers conclusive support for his conspiracy theory, and a WHO team has concluded that it is extremely unlikely that COVID-19 escaped from the Wuhan lab. Furthermore, other experts in virology and biology have stated that the virus shows no signs of genetic manipulation.[11]

Another popular COVID-19 conspiracy theory asserts that the US created COVID-19 and used it as a bioweapon to attack China.[11] This theory was started by Igor Nikulin, a four-time failed political candidate who claims to be a biologist and former weapons inspector in Iraq who served on a UN commission on biological and chemical weapons in the 1990s.[11] Nikulin has offered no evidence to support these claims, however, and former UN weapons inspector Richard Butler, for whom Nikulin claims to have worked, has said that he has no memory of Nikulin and that his story sounds "sloppily fabricated, and not credible."[11] Additionally, no UN records have been found to confirm his claims of employment.[11] Nonetheless, Nikulin's conspiracy theory has managed to gain a significant degree of traction since it was first voiced in a story by Zvezda, a state media outlet tied to the Russian military, in January 20, 2020.[11] Once the virus reached the US, Nikulin revised his theory, asserting that the true culprits are "globalists" using the virus to depopulate the earth.[11] Like Boyle, Nikulin has no evidence to support his claims, and the theory that COVID-19 was engineered by the US suffers from the same flaws as the claim that the virus was manufactured by China – namely, the virus's lack of any signs of genetic manipulation.[11] Belief in COVID-19 conspiracy theories have salient societal effects such as decreased institutional trust and reduced support for public health policies such as physical distancing and mask wearing.

Conclusion

Human history is littered with conspiracy theories, as people consistently turn to conspiracies time and time again when faced with a reality that they struggle to fully comprehend. Prominent conspiracy theories that persist to this day include the moon landing conspiracy, conspiracy theories regarding 9/11, the flat earth conspiracy theory, and various conspiracy theories surrounding COVID-19. The popularity of these conspiracy theories is as much about distrust as it is about a lack of education. As Asheley Landrum has noted, conspiracy theories are really "about distrusting authorities and institutions. [It] seems to be based on both a conspiracy mentality and a deeply held belief that looks a lot like religiosity but isn't necessarily specifically tied to a religion."[10] As such, conspiracy theories are likely to remain a prominent phenomenon, and as has always been the case in the past, it is impossible to say what the next big conspiracy will be.

Works Cited

Chapter 1

1. Douglas KM, Uscinski JE, Sutton RM, Cichocka A, Nefes T, Ang CS, et al. Understanding Conspiracy Theories. Polit Psychol. 2019;40(S1):3–35.

2. Stewart K. Paranoia within Reason [Internet]. 1999 [cited 2021 Jul 13]. 454 p. Available from: https://press.uchicago.edu/ucp/books/book/chicago/P/bo3626884.html

3. Wood MJ, Douglas KM. "What about building 7?" A social psychological study of online discussion of 9/11 conspiracy theories. Front Psychol [Internet]. 2013 [cited 2021 Jul 13];4. Available from: https://www.frontiersin.org/articles/10.3389/fpsyg.2013.00409/full

4. Clarke S. Conspiracy Theories and the Internet: Controlled Demolition and Arrested Development. Episteme. 2007 Jun;4(2):167–80.

5. Raymond AK. The 70 Greatest Conspiracy Theories in Pop-Culture History [Internet]. Vulture. 2016 [cited 2021 Jul 11]. Available from: https://www.vulture.com/2016/10/pop-culture-conspiracy-theories-c-v-r.html

6. Rao TSS, Andrade C. The MMR vaccine and autism: Sensation, refutation, retraction, and fraud. Indian J Psychiatry. 2011;53(2):95–6.

7. Pierce R. Research Methods in Politics [Internet]. 1 Oliver's Yard, 55 City Road, London England EC1Y 1SP United Kingdom: SAGE Publications Ltd; 2008 [cited 2021 Jul 11]. Available from: http://methods.sagepub.com/book/research-methods-in-politics

8. van Prooijen J, Douglas KM. Belief in conspiracy theories: Basic principles of an emerging research domain. Eur J Soc Psychol. 2018 Dec;48(7):897–908.

9. Kramer J. Why people latch on to conspiracy theories, according to science [Internet]. Science. 2021 [cited 2021 Jul 11]. Available from: https://www.nationalgeographic.com/science/article/why-people-latch-on-to-conspiracy-theories-according-to-science

Chapter 2

1. Alfred Moore (2016) Conspiracy and Conspiracy Theories in Democratic Politics, Critical Review, 28:1, 1-23, https://doi-org.myaccess.library.utoronto.ca/10.1080/08913811.2016.1178894

2. Clarke, S. (2002). Conspiracy theories and conspiracy theorizing. Philosophy of the Social Sciences, 32, 131–150.

3. Darwin, H., Neave, N., & Holmes, J. (2011). Belief in conspiracy theories. The role of paranormal belief, paranoid ideation and schizotypy. Personality and Individual Differences, 50, 1289–1293.

4. Douglas, K. M., & Sutton, R. M. (2011). Does it take one to know one? Endorsement of conspiracy theories is influenced by personal willingness to conspire. British Journal of Social Psychology, 50, 544–552.

5. Douglas, K.M., Uscinski, J.E., Sutton, R.M., Cichocka, A., Nefes, T., Ang, C.S. and Deravi, F. (2019), Understanding Conspiracy Theories. Political Psychology, 40: 3-35. https://doi-org.myaccess.library.utoronto.ca/10.1111/pops.12568

6. Ellerton, P. (2014, October 5). The ironclad logic of conspiracy theories and how to break it. The Conversation. https://theconversation.com/the-ironclad-logic-of-conspiracy-theories-and-how-to-break-it-31684

7. Fenster, M. (1999). Conspiracy theories: Secrecy and power in American culture. Minneapolis, MN: University of Minnesota Press.

8. Identifying Conspiracy Theories. (2020). European Commission. https://ec.europa.eu/info/live-work-travel-eu/coronavirus-response/fighting-disinformation/identifying-conspiracy-theories_en

9. Jeffrey M. Bale (2007) Political paranoia v. political realism: on distinguishing between bogus conspiracy theories and genuine conspiratorial politics, Patterns of Prejudice, 41:1, 45-60, https://doi-org.myaccess.library.utoronto.ca/10.1080/00313220601118751

10. Jolley, D., & Douglas, K. M. (2014a). The social consequences of conspiracism: Exposure to conspiracy theories decreases the intention to engage in politics and to reduce one's carbon footprint. British Journal of

Psychology, 105, 35–56.

11. Jolley, D., & Douglas, K. M. (2014b). The effects of anti-vaccine conspiracy theories on vaccination intentions. PLoS ONE, 9(2), e89177

12. Karen M. Douglas, Robbie M. Sutton, Mitchell J. Callan, Rael J. Dawtry & Annelie J. Harvey (2016) Someone is pulling the strings: hypersensitive agency detection and belief in conspiracy theories, Thinking & Reasoning, 22:1, 57-77, https://doi-org.myaccess.library.utoronto.ca/10.1080/13546783.2015.1051586

13. Kramer, Jillian. (2021, January 8), Why people latch on to conspiracy theories, according to science. National Geographic. https://www.nationalgeographic.com/science/article/why-people-latch-on-to-conspiracy-theories-according-to-science

14. Krüger F. (2016) Study II: The Confirmation/Disconfirmation-Paradigm in a Cross-Cultural Perspective – A Study across Countries. In: The Influence of Culture and Personality on Customer Satisfaction. International Management Studies. Springer Gabler, Wiesbaden. https://doi-org.myaccess.library.utoronto.ca/10.1007/978-3-658-12557-8_4

15. McCauley, C. M. (2013, August, 24). Towson author writes a history of conspiracy theories in America. The Baltimore Sun. https://www.baltimoresun.com/entertainment/arts/bs-ae-book-walker-20130824-story.html

16. Miller, S. (2002). Conspiracy theories: public arguments as coded social critiques. Argumentation and Advocacy, 39, 40–56.

17. Swami, V., & Coles, R. (2010). The truth is out there: Belief in conspiracy theories. The Psychologist, 23, 560–563.

18. Treen, Kathie & Williams, Hywel & O'Neill, Saffron. (2020). Online misinformation about climate change. WIREs Climate Change. https://doi-org.myaccess.library.utoronto.ca/10.1002/wcc.665

19. Wikipedia contributors. (2021, July 9). Conspiracy theory. In Wikipedia, The Free Encyclopedia. Retrieved 11:44, July 11, 2021, from https://en.wikipedia.org/w/index.php?title=Conspiracy_theory&oldid=1032687037

20. Wikipedia contributors. (2021, July 13). Project MKUltra. In Wikipedia, The Free Encyclopedia. Retrieved 13:25, July 14, 2021, from https://en.wikipedia.org/w/index.php?title=Project_MKUltra&oldid=1033458563

Chapter 3

1. (N.d.). Google.Com. Retrieved July 17, 2021, from https://books.google.com/ngrams/graph?content=fake+news&year_start=2000&year_end=2019&corpus=26&smoothing=3

2. bias. (n.d.). Dictionary.Com. Retrieved July 17, 2021, from https://www.dictionary.com/browse/bias

3. Berkowitz, D., & Schwartz, D. A. (2016). Miley, CNN andThe Onion: When fake news becomes realer than real. Journalism Practice, 10(1), 1–17.

4. Bakir, V., & McStay, A. (2018). Fake News and The Economy of Emotions: Problems, causes, solutions. Digital Journalism, 6(2), 154–175.

5. First Draft. (2017, February 16). Fake news. It's complicated. First Draft Footnotes. https://medium.com/1st-draft/fake-news-its-complicated-d0f773766c79

6. Berman, D. S., & Stoddard, J. D. (2021). "it's a growing and serious problem:" teaching 9/11 to combat misinformation and conspiracy theories. Social Studies (Philadelphia, Pa.: 1953), 1–12.

7. Riley, A. (2018). 9/11 myths, Islam, and American cultural conflict. Society, 55(4), 329–332.

8. Romer, D., & Jamieson, K. H. (2020). Conspiracy theories as barriers to controlling the spread of COVID-19 in the U.S. Social Science & Medicine (1982), 263(113356), 113356.

9. HealthAnalytics. (2021, May 27). WhatsApp forward claiming 'Vaccinated People Will Die in 2 Years' is untrue - Health Analytics Asia. Ha-Asia.Com. https://www.ha-asia.com/whatsapp-forward-claiming-vaccinated-people-will-die-in-2-years-is-untrue/

10. Kalra, P. (2018). The Silk Road and the Political Economy

of the Mongol Empire (1st ed., Vol. 1). Routledge. https://doi.
org/10.4324/9781315226453

Chapter 4

1. Douglas, K.M., Sutton, R.M., Cichocka, A. (2017). The Psychology
of Conspiracy Theories. Sage Journals, 26(6), 538-542. https://doi.
org/10.1177/0963721417718261

2. New School of Psychotherapy and Counselling. (2018). What is the
Existential Approach. NSPC. https://www.nspc.org.uk/about-the-school/
the-existential-approach/

3. Spear, Jane. (2018). Existential Psychology: History of the movement.
Psychology Jrank. https://psychology.jrank.org/pages/229/Existential-
Psychology.html

Chapter 5

1. Douglas KM, Sutton R, Cichocka A. Belief. Belief in Conspiracy
Theories: Looking Beyond Gullibility. In: Forgas, J.P., Baumeister, R.F.,
editor. The social psychology of gullibility: fake news, conspiracy theories,
and irrational beliefs. New York: London Routledge, Taylor et Francis
Group; 2019. p. 61–76.

2. Douglas KM, Sutton R. Why conspiracy theories matter: A social
psychological analysis. European Review of Social Psychology.
2018;29(1):256-298.

3. Douglas KM, Uscinski JE, Sutton RM, Cichocka A, Nefes T, Ang CS,
et al. Understanding conspiracy theories. Polit Psychol. 2019;40(S1):3–35.

4. Scott S. Negotiating identity: Symbolic interactionist approaches to
social identity: Symbolic interactionist approaches to social identity. 1st ed.
Oxford, England: Polity Press; 2015.

5. Sternisko A, Cichocka A, Van Bavel JJ. The dark side of social
movements: social identity, non-conformity, and the lure of conspiracy
theories. Curr Opin Psychol. 2020;35:1–6.

6. van Prooijen J-W. The psychology of conspiracy theories. London,

England: Routledge; 2018.

7. van Prooijen J-W, Douglas KM. Conspiracy theories as part of history: The role of societal crisis situations. Mem Stud. 2017;10(3):323–33.

8. van Prooijen J-W, Douglas KM. Belief in conspiracy theories: Basic principles of an emerging research domain. Eur J Soc Psychol. 2018;48(7):897–908.

Chapter 6

1. Latifi F. The 9 most popular conspiracy theories in recent history [Internet]. Teen Vogue. 2021 [cited 2021 Jul 13]. Available from: https://www.teenvogue.com/story/most-popular-conspiracy-theories

2. Godwin R. One giant ... lie? Why so many people still think the moon landings were faked. The guardian [Internet]. 2019 Jul 10 [cited 2021 Jul 13]; Available from: http://www.theguardian.com/science/2019/jul/10/one-giant-lie-why-so-many-people-still-think-the-moon-landings-were-faked

3. Howell E. Moon-landing hoax still lives on, 50 years after Apollo 11. But why? [Internet]. Space.com. Space; 2019 [cited 2021 Jul 13]. Available from: https://www.space.com/apollo-11-moon-landing-hoax-believers.html

4. Dickson EJ. A brief history of conspiracy theories about the moon landing [Internet]. Rollingstone.com. Rolling Stone; 2019 [cited 2021 Jul 13]. Available from: https://www.rollingstone.com/culture/culture-features/moon-landing-conspiracy-theories-explained-861205/

5. Jennings R. Moon landing 50th anniversary: why people like Steph Curry have supported conspiracy theories [Internet]. Vox. 2019 [cited 2021 Jul 13]. Available from: https://www.vox.com/the-goods/2019/6/24/18692080/moon-landing-50th-anniversary-steph-curry-conspiracy-theory-hoax

6. Graff GM. 9/11 and the rise of the new conspiracy theorists. Wall Street journal (Eastern ed) [Internet]. 2020 Sep 10 [cited 2021 Jul 13]; Available from: https://www.wsj.com/articles/9-11-and-the-rise-of-the-new-conspiracy-theorists-11599768458

7. 5 compelling 9/11 conspiracy theories [Internet]. History.co.uk. [cited

2021 Jul 13]. Available from: https://www.history.co.uk/shows/road-to-911/articles/5-compelling-911-conspiracy-theories

8. Mirsky S. Flat earthers: What they believe and why. Scientific American [Internet]. 2020 Mar 27 [cited 2021 Jul 13]; Available from: https://www.scientificamerican.com/podcast/episode/flat-earthers-what-they-believe-and-why/
9. The Flat Earth Society [Internet]. Theflatearthsociety.org. [cited 2021 Jul 13]. Available from: https://www.theflatearthsociety.org/home/index.php/about-the-society

10. Author N. Fighting flat-Earth theory – physics world [Internet]. Physicsworld.com. 2020 [cited 2021 Jul 13]. Available from: https://physicsworld.com/a/fighting-flat-earth-theory/

11. The Associated Press, David Klepper FAABD. The superspreaders behind top COVID-19 conspiracy theories [Internet]. CTV News. 2021 [cited 2021 Jul 13]. Available from: https://www.ctvnews.ca/health/coronavirus/the-superspreaders-behind-top-covid-19-conspiracy-theories-1.5309422

www.ingramcontent.com/pod-product-compliance
Lightning Source LLC
Chambersburg PA
CBHW030854270326
41928CB00008B/1364